GOOSE PÂTÉ

A Collection of Short Stories

New Atlantic Media
Chapel Hill, NC
2022

GOOSE PÂTÉ

GOOSE FEDDERS

FOR DANNY

Book Design by Tim Hubbard
New Atlantic Media
Chapel Hill, NC
NewAtlanticMedia2002@gmail.com

10 9 8 7 6 5 4 3 2
ISBN: 978-0-578-10349-5 (Paperback)

Printed in the United States of America

CONTENTS

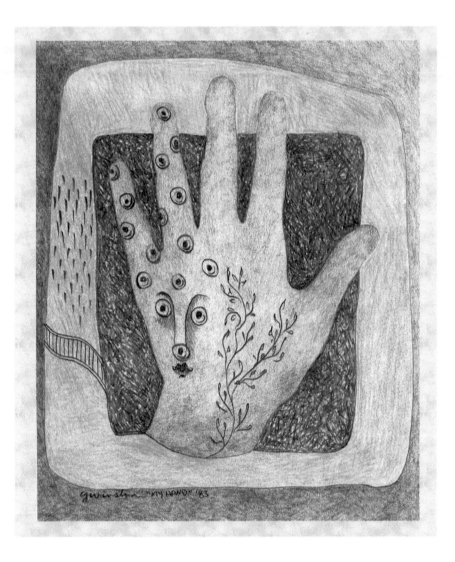

ACKNOWLEDGEMENTS

Thank you, Anne Valley Fox, for your kind encouragement in many endeavors, through decades of friendship and your shining example of doing, not saying, most of that time.

Thank you, Haila Harvey, for the great fun of hatching the egg of "Tame Yo' Hog" on a road trip long ago.

Thank you, Lucy Moore, for your directive of "Do it!" and your own inspiring work.

Thank you, Margaret Keith Clemson, for never, ever, giving up on me.

Finally, thank you, Tim Hubbard and New Atlantic Media, for all your help and expertise in putting this book together, making it an interesting and fun project and publishing these stories.

ETERNAL SHOPPER

T he day my mother died she was lying in her
bedroom on white satin sheets looking out over
the pinon hills to the west. It was late afternoon, the
day was waning and we all sensed this would be her last
sunset. Her four children, nurse and husband bustled
about the room, doing what could be done. She was
lucid and beautiful, her fine skin clear and translucent,
green eyes with lashes as black as ever framing them,
blonde hair fluffy. After a year's battle with two kinds
of uterine cancer she still looked twenty years younger
than she was and still qualified as a great beauty, just as
she had from the age of about twelve. "SHE WAS FROM
FT. WORTH, BUT FT. WORTH COULDN'T HOLD
HER – HER DREAMS WERE AS BIG AS THE TEXAS
SKY," as the song goes, and she transformed herself from

GOOSE PÂTÉ

a depression farmer's daughter to a bejeweled patron of many fine stores. *Mother & Daughter*

She married three times, advised me on my wedding day never to wear anything whiter than my teeth, warned me that single bathrooms cause divorces, and believed all a girl really needs to know how to cook is hollandaise.

I got a warm, prickly feeling suddenly as I crossed the room, a feeling familiar from childhood. I looked around and her eyes were on me, her pale hand came up from the fur coverlet and waved me over. I put my head down to hear as she spoke low: "Honey, that necklace just DOES NOT GO with that outfit." she said slowly. I looked at her with horror. Looking bad was the worst possible crime in her book. Much of my childhood had been spent standing still, arms raised slightly for fittings for clothes. By sixth grade I had a standing weekly hairdresser appointment and tiny high heels. By high school we girls were not allowed to come to the breakfast table without our "faces on" (make-up and sprayed hairdo). One room of the house was a "beauty shop" with a professional chair hairdryer and manicure equipment. Looking bad was a SIN.

I dashed into her dressing room with the television in front of the treadmill, past the two-room closet with floor to ceiling shoe racks and special section for furs and leather, to the lighted bank of mirrors which surrounded her dressing table, a long counter filled with crystal bottles of perfumes and cosmetics, scarves and fine soaps. Near her chair stood a four foot tall jewelry case. I picked a necklace out and put it on. In the previous years the four of us had gathered in this room, visiting with mother. It was always the same: she sat in her silk chair facing the curving bank of mirrors, perfecting her face and hair and choosing jewelry while chatting with us, she glanced at us from time to time in the mirror, standing behind her. Talking to her back while gazing at her face in the mirror did not seem odd to us, we'd done it all our lives. We'd all learned early how to "air-kiss" so as not to muss the make-up or hair, to stand on tiptoe and approach slowly so as not to scuff her shoes, hands at sides, no lunging or sticky kisses.

Mother didn't like noisy, slimy, smelly, shiny (for unknown reasons) or sticky things.

I went back into the bedroom, wearing the new necklace and shortly had that warm prickly feeling that my mother's eyes were on me again. I leaned in close to hear her whisper her last words to me: "That's much better. Thanks."

The sun sank shortly into the mountains in an orange blaze, and an hour later the Belle of Ft. Worth sank into her final coma, while speaking clearly to an unseen companion: "Well, I don't know, do you think he'd like that? The color is just right but that paisley is a knockout ... I think I'll buy that one and a couple of the gold ones ...." It brought a whole new depth to the phrase "SHOP TIL YOU DROP."

My mother, the Eternal Shopper, dwells in that Great Big Department Store in the sky now, dressing for the gods.

ELECTRIC SISTER

Electra Lynne came out hollering with her white hair sticking straight out as if lightning had struck her and wide eyes of the pale electric green which outlines a storm cloud on the plains. Her voice was piercing as a crack of thunder and her energy wild as a tornado touching down.

And why not? She came into being the night our parents decided to die together.

They'd been to Ft. Worth, a couple of hours away by car, to go to the Texas State Fair. There was nothing noteworthy about the state fair that year except the incident at the Chicken on the Run booth. They'd waited twenty minutes in line and just as Daddy stepped up to the counter the man put a sign in the window saying Back in 15 Minutes. It made him mad and twenty minutes later when they were strolling by there again and the booth was open with no traffic he called out to the guy "Hey, you got any chicken over there?" "Yes Sir!" the man beamed, and our father loudly announced where he could put his fried chicken.

In the back seat of the car was a two foot tall plaster statue of Popeye for me. A sandstorm came up on

their way home and worsened into a thunderstorm and then a rainstorm so violent Daddy could no longer see the road or hold to it when the wind came up so hard, so he pulled over. Just as he came to a halt the electric phone pole in front of the car crashed down six feet ahead of the headlights. Two minutes later the pole behind the car came down, and the high-power lines between those poles draped themselves over the car, with arcs of electric fire shooting between them. To the side of the driver's window two lines slacked. They could see that a foot away from the door they would have to climb over one and under another wire almost simultaneously. The handles on the door of the car were metal. Clearly, the chances of getting out without being electrocuted were not good, and staying inside, with the unpredictable fiery arcs between the wires which might blow against the car or start an electrical fire any moment, was just as deadly. A police car went by, saw the electrical display over the car and noted the license plate before he crawled forward into the storm. On reaching our home town thirty miles away the cops traced this information and located the next of kin to inform them the car had been spotted and no survivors were expected. Heartbroken, they waited for a final confirmation before coming over to tell us were orphans.

Meanwhile, back in the car illuminated with great bolts of lightning and giant cracks of thunder and a howling tornado wind, our twenty year old mother and forty year old father talked things over and when our father explained that he might be electrocuted when he touched the door handle and began to tell her what she should do next she began to cry and insist that she wanted to die with him, and he wept and admitted he had rather die than live without her either. They decided to die together and this led to a last long passionate embrace of unforeseen consequences before they clasped hands and our father reached for the door handle. Together they climbed out, over one wire and under another, struggled to the highway and caught a ride to town. When they got home, soaked to the bone and laughing with joy at being alive, they called their relatives, who had been waiting to identify their charred bodies, to tell about their amazing adventure. The car was towed in the following morning with not a chip on my Popeye statue, and nine months later our beautiful electric sister was born.

WHY WE STOLE AUNT CLYDE

S he was born around the turn of the last century to St. Louis socialites, an only child. They'd expected a boy and decided on giving her the name they had already chosen: Clyde Horace Beedle. She was, perhaps in consequence, an artistic, intellectual free spirit all her days. Aunt Clyde painted, wrote, danced and laughed her way through life in her beloved Santa Fe. She did not give gifts at Christmas or on birthdays, but would send a surprise gift box when you least expected and most needed it – say on a dreary cold January day or blowing March morning. Surprise gifts are known in the family today as "Aunt Clydes."

Clyde wore peasant blouses and broomstick skirts with ballet slippers, bright red lipstick and nail polish, with berets from Suzette's, which exactly matched her long cigarette holders, and she painted everything aqua. She was somewhat Bohemian, and received Rosicrucian and Free Thinking literature in the mail regularly. After her passing, I found a large stash of morning glory seeds in a box deep in her closet, and, putting that together with the fact that no morning glories were growing in her gardens, discerned that she had put together a hoard of unsprayed seeds for tripping on. When she painted she wore a blue cotton French painter's smock, which exactly matched her eyes. She had pale ash-blonde curls and no eyebrows since plucking them off in the 1930's movie star style, so she drew on rather dramatic ones, which changed from day to day, much like herself.

Her husband was our Uncle T.I. Johnson. His nickname was Blue Sky, a sly dig at his wild entrepreneurial ideas. He was a wild-catter, a trader, dandy and inventor. Never seen without a beautiful suit, his diamond stickpin and a fresh flower – usually a red rosebud – in his lapel, he also walked a slack wire daily. The slack wire, only about six inches off the ground, can pitch you six feet and is quite hard to master, as our bruises attested, but he was perfectly balanced on it even at ninety. He set up his slack wire at the hotels he stayed in when he traveled and small crowds gathered to watch him walk it, trim and light-footed. Onlookers were always invited to try it but we never saw anyone else walk it more than a few wildly swinging steps before they landed on their backs in the grass. We were wild to have one of our own but mother nixed it: too dangerous!

He invented Mistallax, a medicine so vile tasting we kids would deny a stomach ache to avoid taking it – but which actually did as he claimed, seem to cure whatever ailed you. Naturally, the Food and Drug Administration was both curious and skeptical, so Mistallax has remained a bootleg item. He had a pamphlet praising the wonders of Mistallax with a testimonial in it by a grandmother named Fanny Strong, and believe me you needed a name like that to take the stuff. Wherever Blue Sky traveled he sold his snake oil medicine, which was actually water from a well on the old home place with a high mineral content boiled down into an oily yellow dose of salts. In his hotel room there would be a display: a small table set up with a white fancy cloth, a single red rose in a bud vase and a pile of the pamphlets. We had to keep a stash of it out in the washhouse for customers who ran out of it before he came back through town. The old folks told us we were lucky; it was better than the castor oil they'd had to take, but it never increased our appreciation a bit.

Uncle Blue Sky loved to talk, telling tall tales of his own adventures, pausing only to relight his cigar, with his diamond rings twinkling in the flame from his gold butane lighter. Every story ended with the free advice to Buy a Packard Car and a lecture on the virtues of Packard cars, second only to Mistallax in his view. It was a mistake to mention that Packard cars were not being made anymore, for the long explosion which followed would eventually reveal a government conspiracy you'd be sworn to secrecy on, so I can not tell you about that.

Aunt Clyde had heard about Packard Cars, government conspiracies and Fanny Strong many, many times by the time she died and went to what she hopefully called "The Big Quiet."

For years it bothered us that Uncle Blue Sky did not honor her final request to scatter her ashes, but kept them in the ugly tin from the mortuary under her pillow and, unlike before her death, talked to her every night for as long as he liked, and even longer as the years passed. T.I. Blue Sky always said he'd live to be one hundred and twenty three years old but he died two weeks short of one hundred with his party all planned and his jet black hair just beginning to silver around the ears.

We were his blood relatives and trusted houseguests, but at long last one fine spring day when the sky was exactly the blue of Aunt Clyde's eyes and her big old favorite apricot tree had just burst into bloom, and the thought of her free spirit trapped in a can was too terrible to endure any longer, we carefully pried that can open. It was at this point that the complexity of the criminal life began to evidence itself. The ingredients of the can were natural ingredients not easy to duplicate from the gravel in the driveway and greenery of the yard, and the motley assembly had to SOUND RIGHT. This took some effort and concentration, adding a few things to the can and then shaking it, getting a consensus before adding another tiny pebble and trying again, which is probably why we didn't notice Socorro, Uncle's faithful longtime housekeeper, approaching from the street until it was almost too late to pretend to be picking flowers and dashing inside to put them in a vase. Once inside my mother and sister got the top back on the can and began desperately tossing the hot-potato funerary container back and forth between them: HERE, YOU TAKE IT AND RUN.

NO, YOU TAKE IT AND HIDE and so on until Mother pulled rank and ordered my sister to GET IT OUT OF THE HOUSE NOW, whereupon I tossed a shopping bag at sister, who dropped the can into it and was out the door, strolling innocently past the approaching Socorro with a cheery wave.

And she almost made it full away before the can dropped down inside the shopping bag onto a purchase we'd made earlier – a laughing box. As bad luck would have it the can fell straight onto the lever and set off the deep laughing voice inside the box. My sister, recognized by our mother as the only one with an ounce of natural dignity, upheld the faith, walking straight-faced and straight forward into the street, seemingly unaware of being surrounded by invisible booming laughter - and around the corner, where we joined her as soon as Socorro went inside the house, looking bewildered. We waited for the innocent woman to leave, and did what we had to do.

We could hardly breathe that night until Uncle Blue Sky could be heard droning on as usual telling Aunt Clyde's ashes to corner the market on copper pipe and buy a Packard Car. Then we smiled at each other, for Aunt Clyde was safely outside in a thin circle beneath her apricot tree and the stars, except for the tiny puff of ashes we saw take off in a sudden Santa Fe breeze, heading towards the Sangre de Cristo mountains.

WATERMELON SEEDS

Mary Nell's first food fancy was watermelon; the cool crispness both banished the summer heat for her, and mollified her sweet tooth in the middle of the night, when she would tiptoe into the kitchen after she woke up too hot and scoop a big hunk out of a melon sitting in the icebox with a large silver serving spoon, and eat it in the dark, slurping up the juice so it wouldn't run down onto her cotton nightie. She rinsed her hands silently and ran her wet fingers through her hair to dry them.

When she and her mother went together to Kouri's grocery store, she would always ask for a watermelon and her mother would tell the butcher, Sammy, who would wash his hands and long knife and motion them into the back room. This room was dim, with a cold stone floor where the biggest melons stood. Together they would thump a few and pick one which sounded hollow but not so hollow-sounding as to be "over the line," and Sammy would nod and make a long triangular cut and pull out the plug for inspection, the tip of it being a sample of the very center of the fruit. Her mother would give the butcher a twinkly little smile as if to say "we'll take it" but instead she said to Mary Nell, "Would you taste it for me?" and Mary "Watermelon" Nell was happy to oblige. Sammy would slice off that best bit and put in right into her mouth. After her approval, he would put the plug back in and lift it up in his big arms to carry to the car. Watermelon only cost a few cents a pound and a large one, enough for all the kids with some left over, might be two dollars or three. Nevertheless, melons were judged by the strictest rules and people were endlessly picky about their summer treat: they had to be perfect. There were three kinds Mary Nell knew of: dark green with dark red meat and striped green ones which were bright red inside, and the yellow ones, which were even sweeter and not as available. The store seldom carried them, but a few local farmers grew yellow watermelons, which could be found in season at fruit stands out in the countryside. They were a special treat, like pickled watermelon rinds in the winter.

When supper was over - just plain old fried chicken, mashed potatoes, green beans, sliced tomatoes, fried okra, biscuits, cream gravy and little pickled crabapples - no dessert because it was a watermelon night - and the long summer evening rolled towards dusk, the chilled melon would be brought out and sliced open with the great cracking sound the first cut makes, falling open of its own weight onto the old wooden picnic table in the back yard. By then the children would have all their clothes off and be sitting naked on an old quilt on the grass. Their mother was an efficient housekeeper who had discovered that the least messy way to feed watermelon to children was without clothes, and then to hose them down afterwards on the grass. This meant they could get completely sticky and squirt watermelon seeds at each other until the stars and lightning bugs came out, until the garden hose gushed wet and cold and all the kids screamed and danced in the chilly spray before they were rubbed down with big warm towels and put to bed. For all her early years she thought that everyone ate watermelon in this manner.

Mary Nell, like her sisters, had been well-trained when guests arrived to answer the door, greet them warmly, show them into the den, and ask what they would like to drink. One silly friend of their family always asked for "just a big old glass of yellow-meated watermelon juice" to tease them. He claimed he drank it everyday and it ought to be available. The girls would have to apologize and get a second choice out of him, which wasn't easy. He'd finally accept something, saying sadly he'd just have to take "whatever" if he couldn't have what he wanted. After several summers of this, the man finally happened to come by on a day when a yellow watermelon was actually cooling in the box, and he made his usual request. Mary Nell and her sister barely held their giggles until they got to the kitchen, where together they cut the melon and with their small hands squeezed great chunks out of the center over a strainer into a big glass, filled it with ice and topped it off with a sprig of mint from the bed outside the back door by the hose, and delivered it to the man on a small silver tray. His face was a study as he solemnly thanked them and drank it down. They stood primly watching as he drank - there was no escape for him. They'd waited years of their short lives for this sight, a man drinking yellow-meated watermelon juice as if he did it every day. Their Dad came in just then, saw the finish of the performance and roared with laughter each of the three times the man had to go pee in the hour before he left the house, and the next time the man came he said he just wanted a whiskey and soda.

When Mary Nell was ten she was downtown with her mother, crossing a street - her mother still held her hand when crossing a street - when a woman passed by. She was very, very big in her middle, like a tadpole! "Mommy!" Mary Nell cried out "What is the matter with that lady?"

"Shhhh!" her mother hissed, tightening her grip on Mary's wrist and walking faster. In those days pregnant women stayed inside during their third trimester as a matter of delicacy and safety, and were seldom seen out on the street. Even at home a woman might just wear looser clothes and not mention a baby coming to her children. Mary Nell knew that women had some mysterious disorder called PG. She had heard them whisper to each other "I think I'm PG" or "Margie is PG for sure." Mary

Nell's mother was annoyed, downtown daylight was not the time for explanations of this nature. Besides she had read The Little Book to Mary Nell the night before her first day in school, when she was six, in case the child might "hear things" on the playground. The Little Book explained procreation in terms of flowers, bees, and fruit, complete with stamens and pistils. When she had finished reading it to her, alone in the bedroom with the door locked in case the other children were listening, she asked Mary Nell if she understood and Mary Nell had said "Yes, Ma'm." Thank goodness, that was settled and her duty had been done. So now she said to Mary Nell in a low voice, "Hush and don't stare. She swallowed a watermelon seed."

That night the girl dreamed that she herself had swallowed a watermelon seed and saw long twisting dark green vine tendrils coming out of her ears and leaves on the vines beginning to uncurl while her stomach swelled up, and she woke up in a sweat. The next time she ate watermelon she couldn't enjoy it for worrying about accidentally swallowing a seed, and she had the exact same dream again that night, so she claimed watermelon gave her a stomachache (not exactly a lie, which was a sin for which she might go to Hell) and gave it up for good. The next time she saw a pregnant woman she had the dream again, and even after she finally managed to connect bees and fruit to human sex and babies, she could not forget the miserable notion of having a watermelon grow inside herself, of connecting the two and avoiding both.

Seed Jar

By the time she was thirty-five and a spinster working on her Masters' degree in Library Science, Mary Nell had missed much of life's sweetness due to watermelon seeds. That summer, however, she attended a school picnic, and while she was sitting on a quilt spread out on the grass and overlooking the river on a hot August day, a long cool shadow fell over her. A man approached from the potluck table with the sun behind him, carefully carrying a big white china plate.

"Hello, Miss," he said quietly, "I've been wanting to make your acquaintance, and I noticed you didn't get any dessert, so I've brought you some." On the plate was a big cut of yellow watermelon, the small black seeds studding the sides like evil missiles ready to launch. "Oh, NO. Thank you. I don't care for watermelon seeds." She had meant to say watermelon, but "seeds" just slipped out, so of course he said, "Well, Ma'm, you eat the other part. And what could you possibly have against watermelon seeds?" Her face got hot and before she could stop herself she said, "You don't want to know," too embarrassed to pretend not to be.

"Sure I do." he answered, sitting down with that watermelon plate between them, a silver fork sticking out and a cloth napkin underneath.

So she told him the whole story and he didn't laugh. He said, "Well, those seeds aren't all bad. I bet I know something about them you don't know." He pinched one little seed out of the melon. "Put this seed on the tip of your tongue, close your mouth and press the seed up just behind your front teeth. Breathe in and then out, and when you do, you'll hear the ocean."

She tried it and she did hear the ocean, then she spit the seed out, and while they ate the melon together, she told him the story of the man who drank yellow-meated watermelon juice as if he did it every day, and he did laugh. She was thirty-five then, as I mentioned, and they had four children by the time she was forty-one, and in no time at all they were eating watermelon naked in the back yard.

MY HAIR

I've begun reading Mark Twain's autobiography and am inspired to begin my own even though at his insistence I am thirty years late – Twain says you must begin at forty.

Furthermore, Twain planned to 'draw portraits' of all the loads of famous people he knew with snappy words. I've known very few famous people – and none of them well – except myself, and I was only famous to myself. Always starring in my own movie, I was! And right off the bat I was the center of me own world, ready at all times for my close-up. At the worst of times I considered camera angles, lighting. Never have I been too shocked, terrified, ill, endangered or destitute not to consider my appearance.

When my first baby was born by caesarian (for no good reason except that I was nervous about natural childbirth and had a doctor all too willing to accommodate that in order to keep his own schedule tidy), something went awry with the saddle-block anesthetic. The two surgeons my doc had called in were, I kid you not, Dr. Slaughter and Dr. Tremble. They both noticed something was not right when Tremble began to slice open my ripe belly and I screamed STOP!

You can't feel that, the surgeon snapped. YES, I CAN I insisted. Slaughter stepped up with a needle and mumbled Just let me check something here and proceeded to jab it into my big toe. I yelled OUCH! He tried the other big toe and I hollered QUIT IT! They looked at each other and went into a quick huddle while I considered saying Goddammit if they needled another, but I knew I wouldn't. My baby would be born soon and I didn't want him to hear me cussing right away. Besides, it was a small town and everything got out and someone would tell my mother, who was already plenty mad at me.

But Slaughter and Tremble didn't do that – they came out of their huddle and talked to me, talked a lot faster than usual: We think the anesthesia went through your spine instead of into it. We gotta operate and we don't have time to give you any more stuff. You gotta hang on. We have only ten minutes to get the baby out before the anesthetic gets to the baby. See that clock on the wall? Concentrate on it!

A nurse I'd known since childhood was called quickly in, a makeshift screen put up between my face and belly, a hand towel flung over an aluminum frame. It was white with a green stripe which read Bethania Hospital. The nurse took my hand, Slaughter said Ready and I turned my face to the clock high on the green wall, figuring I'd just pass out from the pain like cowboys did in the movies during outback amputations, but I didn't. No such luck. I sweated, which was a big-time beauty no-no. The doctors were making short zig-zag type cuts, unused to cutting up a flinching, awake person and each cut stung like a thousand bee stings at once. Then the scalpel tip started again at the top and went deeper and there was a sudden gush of – I don't know what – blood and piss was my nicest guess – some sort of fluid and the damp place under me started to soak upward on the operating table, towards my long naturally curly auburn hair which I'd just washed that morning so I'd look good while I had my baby.

Bodily fluids, which I was not into, were creeping, squishing, up beneath me to my shoulders and soon would be in my hair. The clock showed five minutes gone by. I just knew things weren't going well but on the flip side it dawned on me that I probably wasn't going to die if I was worried about my hair. This got me through the next long, long five minutes during which both surgeons got their hands stuck inside me trying to lift the baby out, struggling against a suction factor they also hadn't counted on.

At long last the baby popped out and I caught a glimpse of a red-haired boy they held up triumphantly for me to see just before they finally knocked me out.

In my long life since then, in time of crisis, I chose to worry about my hair instead of whatever else was going on. Things generally sorted themselves out while I was doing that. A young and rather silly girl entered that operating room, but a wiser one was wheeled out.

Down There

My grandmother, Mama Ree, did not know about the courtship of her only daughter until she noticed that her bill for wooden matches had risen on the monthly tally from the general store. Determined to solve this mystery, she finally located her girl at midnight on the back porch in the dark lighting one match after another while the train rambled through. A blinking lantern light echoed those lit matches from the train. A young brakeman had taken pursuit of the tall light-haired, blue-eyed girl. They were married in a few months, Nona Ree being rather shy and reserved and Raymond Dean Booker in a lustful hurry.

Nona Ree had no idea what to expect from marriage or "love." The subject was not discussed at home, but she knew enough to fear pregnancy and asked the older women outright how to avoid babies and they told her there was no way that they knew of except to nurse each baby a long time, so she could perhaps get more time in between babies. She told her fiancee she did not want babies right away and he wore a rubber condom on their wedding night when she did her new wifely duty. The next day she was bathing in a washtub when some pieces of rubber fell out of her vagina, frightening her. She had in good Victorian fashion covered her eyes with her hands during the act itself, and she became fearful and refused to allow sex again with her new husband, but nine months to the day after her wedding she went into labor with her baby in breech position. Three agonizing days and nights later she was finally delivered of little Raybo. She promptly put her baby in the bed between herself and her husband and proceeded to nurse Raybo for the next six years, until his frustrated and still-hopeful father promised him a pair of red cowboy boots if he would quit. Raybo took the deal and moved out of the bedroom.

Nona Ree had come into herself enough to refuse her husband sex anyhow, fearing pregnancy more than ever and still terrified by her experience. She grew quite fat and bossy while her husband, now known as Poppy Dean, appeared to shrink beside her. When television came to town she gave up listening to the radio all day long and while she watched, she embroidered tea towels in cross stitch with the names of the days of the week twined 'round with daisies and greenery. Her only other vice besides smoking and Phenobarbitol, according to Mama Ree, was reading dime novel paperbacks with lurid covers. "Sister's gone kill somebody someday," her mother used to warn us children. Elephantine herself, Nona Ree collected elephants, which faced the front door in perfect order, trunks upraised, from the mantle over the fireplace with the gas stove in it. With her long red fingernails each morning she laid out the cigarettes she intended to smoke that day on the keys of her piano. She played the piano well and dominoes badly, cried and pitched a terrible fit whenever she lost, so that even we children schemed to lose the game to her. For whomever picked up the ringing phone, the raspy voice of Aunt Nona Ree was the worst possible immediate future; we had our orders of civility.

With four aching, boisterous teenagers in the house there was great jostling to get any call, involving leaps and gymnastic dodges and twirls towards the instrument of such desire and news. We'd come far from the day when the phone rang and our younger brother blurted out to our mother – the only one allowed to answer the phone: "If that's Miz McCutchen, she's a damn liar!"

Nowadays, we were all trained to answer "You have reached the Watson residence, to whom would you like to speak?" A little silence, then, the answer portended by a massive clearing of throat, a garbled deep wheezing announced the dreaded reality: It was Aunt Nona Ree. Mother, seeing the tell-tale expression on the face of the unlucky one, would turn away to hide a smile: she had to run errands for her elderly sister-in-law.

"It's Nona Ree, honey." the answer rumbled up from the depths of two packs of unfiltered Camel cigarettes a day deposited in her ancient lungs. You had to say, then: "How are you, Mam?"

"Aw, honey, my vagina hurts! It is as dry as a bone and driving me crazy....I don't know what to do." Vaginas were in those days referred to as a sort of geographical location known as Down There. Boys had an Outfit, which were mentioned more often than female outfits, which was never. "I just hope you never have to go through anything like this, child. Listen, you keep your windows closed at night, you hear? Or else some old Outfit will crawl up in there and get you!"

"Well, I'm real sorry, Mam. Can I get my mother for you?" and you'd hand over the phone as gingerly as if it were on fire.

It was a fairly dangerous world, even for local princesses, and I often had bad dreams about Giant Outfits walking towards the house on long spindly legs.

We were forbidden to mention outside the family (or in it, for that matter) that Aunt Nona Ree had once set her vagina on fire. It happened in a gas station on the way home from the annual family reunion. We each went to the "can" and Auntie went last. When she finally came out, my father, her youngest brother, began to scold her for taking so much time, and then, sniffing the air indignantly, asked "What's that smell?" Nona Ree set her lips in a tight line and answered "I can't tell you. You forbid me to speak the word." TELL ME ANYWAY! He roared, "Are you all right?"

"Yes," she sniffed back a tear. "I accidentally set my vagina on fire." She went on to explain that just after putting a lot of paper into the toilet she had lit a cigarette and dropped the match into the bowl between her legs and the paper flared up so fast she "didn't have time to get her vagina out of the way" and got "scorched." She added that she was okay, but in no mood to be scolded. After a moment of silence, he said THEN I NEVER WANT TO HEAR ANOTHER WORD ABOUT THIS AND YOU KIDS HAD BETTER FORGET ABOUT IT TOO. In the front seat my mother's head was down and her shoulders were silently shaking, but it did not seem as if she was crying, really. We didn't even look at each other all the way home, but some family memories are just... unforgettable.

THE YEAR I TURNED FIFTEEN

The year I turned fifteen three things happened - well - four: I found out I was adopted, saw Elvis, and told lies on the Ed Sullivan show.

Finding out you were adopted up in your teens was not uncommon in a time when parents were perfect and set shining examples of virtue. Often it did not really mean adopted, but that you were only related by blood to one of your parents. Meaning one of them had made an early mistake and you were it. Only rarely did it mean that you had been outright adopted by strangers and were so loved that they could not bear to have you know about it. They protected adopted kids because usually people did not let go of their kids for any good reason. It meant hard times, sad stories, possibly bad blood. People watched adoptees all their lives with slightly-narrowed eyes, waiting for the unsteadiness to come out. Maybe at about fifty, after raising a large family with no wavering at all, your own folks and/or their neighbors would let it go and decide you had done all right after all so far, praise the Lord and knock on wood. When you were about sixty five or so, they'd mention you'd overcome Lord knows what, or turned out all right in spite of your circumstances, thanks to being adopted. At no time were you given credit for a good character of your own, a depressing aspect and perhaps best not known – but even worse, from the get-go every single person older than yourself in your world knows something you don't about yourself and are lying to you fairly often when stuff comes up. Then some damn fool trips up, spills the beans and no matter what anyone says to you about it, things are never the same, and never quite as good again as the Before.

Well, naturally I got the double whammy: one of my parents had made an early mistake and I was it, and my other, mystery parent was a criminal, slacker and drunk, a veritable barrel of bad blood. They just hated to tell me that, so they didn't, but they loved me, they said. It explained a lot. Like that I was a damn fool to believe them all those years when I wondered why I was short and dark and my siblings were tall and blonde and they said Well, there's a runt in every litter. I asked my grandmother what a runt was. Oh, she answered, flapping the wrinkles out of wet clothes before hanging them on the line. Usually in every litter of animals there is one smaller that the others. The runt often dies or the mother kills it because they're weak, sickly and not worth the.........a sudden change came over her face and a moment passed before she said, in a different tone of voice, Why do you ask? I explained that Mother has said I was the runt of her litter. She pressed her lips together as she did when she needed a moment to get control of herself and then continued to add that also, actually quite often, if the runt is well taken care of, it turns out to be the very best one.

In less than a year my stepfather would come upon me kissing a boy in the back yard, standing up stiffly in broad daylight fully clothed and hardly touching each other – my first kiss, and he roared at the boy and dragged me into the house by my long hair and slammed me across the bed yelling out "Bad blood is bad blood! You can't make a silk purse out of a sow's ear." This is the fourth big thing that happened in my fifteenth year, the one I didn't list because I still don't like to think about it.

He'd given up on my looks years before, announcing when I was about eleven – an underweight, undersize age eleven with an overbite and thick glasses - one night as I drifted off to sleep, he came in to say goodnight during a party, a little tight, and announced in a conversational sort of way that he and my mother had decided not to "do anything" about my face, that my bone structure was indefinite and my chin weak. I already knew that a weak chin was a sign of weak character, having heard him say it. He said they loved me anyway, just the way I am. Then he patted me on the head and walked away. It was quite a while before I got to sleep. Pleasing him had proven to be hard right along. First off, my acting ability had been poor. When he told me to cry for his motion picture camera I didn't, until he spanked me. Then he bought me a present as an apology. I remember I picked out a big toy airplane, pretending I could fly away in it.

The most precious gift I ever got I didn't recognize when I got it. The best gift I ever got was a bald-faced lie.

My mother didn't lie, she just didn't tell me I was

adopted by my father. That's what she said when I asked her. I overheard a conversation between Aunt Lou and Boozer, Daddy's best friend and business partner. They got into an argument about what year my father, Franklin, had married. I'd never known that he had been married to anyone but our mother, so that right there was a big ole crack in the facade of perfection. I'd had feelings over my brief fifteen years that I was too different from my siblings. Over a three day period after hearing the argument in the saloon, during which I refused to eat, the truth came out: Franklin was my stepfather. My mother had a brief teenage marriage. She'd just turned eighteen when I was born. My biological father would remain a mystery for another twenty-five years because nobody would talk to me about it.

Back in my room alone I stared at my notebooks and collection of pictures of Indians. Of all the kids, only I had taken an intense interest in the fact that my father Franklin was one-sixteenth Cherokee, and enormous pride in being part-Cherokee myself. I had collected articles, pictures, read books, done research, interviewed relatives of him, feeling a deep bond there. So – it turns out, I thought bitterly – my dad isn't my dad and I don't possess a single drop of Indian blood and I'm the only one who doesn't and I'd been making a nuisance and a fool of myself to boot, putting everybody on the spot until the truth came out. I burst into tears. The fact of no Indian blood seemed to me the worst of my losses on a bad day.

My grandmother came into my room, and gave me a hug. I told her why I was crying and she gave me another hug and a tissue. Just before she reached the door she stopped, came back and said slowly, in a low voice, Ah, this is sort of a secret but, you know, there is supposed to be Indian blood on my side of the family.

What? I cried. I was amazed. How come you never told me that before?

She looked down at her hands and said most of the old folks didn't like to admit to Indian blood so it just didn't get mentioned much.

WHAT TRIBE? I jumped, grabbing this lifeline out of an identity crisis.

Ah, well, maybe...Apache? I'm not sure....she said and added I've got a pie in the oven as she bustled out the door. Most all her relatives were dead or gone far away so there was no way to fill in the gaps, and I lost interest slowly due to lack of information as time went by, but from that day I felt completed again in knowing I had my own personal stash of Indian blood in common with my grandmother and mother even if it was so far back we didn't show it and nobody remembered anything about it except 'maybe Apache.' My mother never mentioned her Apache blood. Most likely my grandmother never mentioned it to her. It was a family in which many things were not mentioned. And, given my grandmother's long struggle for a more civilized life there was little draw towards recalling forgotten roots.

Lizzie Mae was born in 1901, the first child of John McAllen and Betsy Ann Enroe, nine months to the day after the wedding. Betsy's bridegroom turned out to have a temper matching his wild charm and unrestrained appetites – she would be dead in nine short years at 28, worn out from beatings and five babies in quick succession. Her furious parents buried Betsy in their own churchyard with her maiden name on her tombstone to register their feelings to the world about the loss of their daughter.

Betsy's daughter Lizzie was tall for her age and fought off her daddy not long after her mother died.

She decided it was safer to be outside the house than inside and marched out to work in the fields and barn, becoming an excellent rider and good ranch hand, too valuable and strong to be messed with. She was allowed to go to school through the eighth grade, the highest level at that time, with good marks in spite of the outdoor work and helping her teenaged new stepmother raise six younger siblings and half-siblings in all. Her father, known as Daddy J, used his horse whip often for little or no reason. The night before she married, her father used his riding quirt on her bare back so that she would go to her husband with his marks on her. He did this with each of his daughters. On her wedding day she asked Miss Ellie, her stepmother, if she might use her bar of fancy soap to bathe with, and was refused. She bathed with lye soap and cold water, and she did not cry when the welts stung. She was way too tough for that, and having gotten religion along her rough path she had early on and all by herself forged a sterling character incapable of subterfuge, breaking a commandment, or any other form of sin including dancing. Her moral code was unbreakable and inseparable from herself. She took joy in hard work and educated herself in the finer arts from magazines and books, isolated on ranches and farms most of her life. She did not drink, smoke, cuss or gossip. She disapproved of the word Xmas because it left the Christ out of Christmas. She did sing, hum and whistle but even I understood as a child that it was a form of praying. She was not afraid of anything in this world except the Knights of Columbus, and I have seen her rassle a steer down to the ground without a rope, hoe a six-foot-long rattlesnake into long division, and sew up a goat with her curved upholstery needle. Sick animals, from baby squirrels to brahma bulls got well under her care, and, as she put it herself, whether they wanted to or not. When her magnificent garden gave out she knew where to go to find wild greens, poke salad, watercress and herbs for ailments. When the harvest was in she canned and preserved and dried a generous winters' worth of tasty food, enough for her family and a few people or family members who had not enough to get by on. No one near her went hungry and an extra place was always set at her table. She kept these qualities and this generosity and total honesty to the end of her days, almost ninety years.

Thinking over her life a few months ago, twenty years now since her death – I also suddenly thought of how courageous and sweet she was to admit her Indian blood to make me feel better in the face of her own disapproval. I recalled clearly how she had looked down at her hands, turning them over as she spoke, and right then I knew in a flash of light like she used to describe Glory Day, the fiery end of the world, that she had lied. To make me feel better this true paragon of virtue TOLD A LIE. She knew me inside out; she knew I would never, ever doubt her because she never, ever told a lie. She knew I would believe it as long as I needed to, and that it would make me brave and strong, that fake Apache blood.

But in the Big Picture, as the grown-ups liked to say, we were lucky children and I knew it. Our Daddy wasn't rich but we believed he was and as the song goes on, our mother good-looking and twenty years younger than her handsome, energetic, charismatic, party-boy, traveling-and-gone-half-the-time husband. We lived in a gracious red-brick house with white columns, in a neighborhood of green manicured lawns, big trees, vacant lots, free-roaming pets and apartments over double-car garages and lining the alleyway for help. Like clockwork, every two years the interior walls were painted, a new Cadillac purchased, and the photographer arrived from Dallas to take our family portrait in the same wing-back chairs in the same corner of the living room. These were hung on the opposite wall over the piano in a long row, eventually a total of seven, and when viewed in a scanning mode, gave the impression not so much that we were growing as that our parents were shrinking. I was the secure first child of a glorious couple, with three younger siblings who had to mind me because I was the oldest. Life was just about perfect.

We lived in the City of Churches, Wichita Falls, Texas, with the highest income per capita in the USA at the time – 1957 – aka Tornado Alley, the Bible Belt, and Baja Oklahoma. The Red River runs through it and once upon a time boasted about a five-foot waterfall which was wiped out in a twister but replaced fifty years later after a campaign to Put The Falls Back In Wichita Falls. White settlers were tricked into moving there by the Kickapoos. Here, they signed in the air, The Big Wind never crosses the water. And the settlers settled there and the Big Wind came about three to five times a year and sucked up all the water in the river WHILE crossing it and leveling all human life or signs of habitation and livestock in its path, so the Kickapoos were technically truthful. The survivors were right hardy.

I belonged to the Methodist Youth Foundation, went to Sunday school and then church on Sundays, belonged to the Junior Forum and Spanish club, Fifty-Fashion Favorites and the Yearbook committee, in most of which I was second-vice president, a position involving decorations. I'd been identified as The Artistic One. My designated color was powder blue, to match my eyes. Sister Sue Ellen (secretly the love child and first-born of the glorious couple) was pale pink. Sister Electra, a tow-head, jonquil yellow. Baby Franklin (the II, Daddy skipping the Junior because he didn't like the way it sounded). The Boy had an insurance policy on him and got to wear any color he wanted except the aforementioned feminine colors.

I was a good girl. A virgin to date, and, well, a good girl. I had three best girlfriends and boys were beginning to take notice. I planned to grow up and live there or maybe two whole hours away in Dallas or Ft. Worth (My mother's people were from the Ft. Worth area – more cow people and rowdy. A generation before it had been the Whore Capital of The Southwest. Her bad old grandaddy was known as the meanest man in Tarrant County. His own mules would back up into a corner and tremble at his approach. Dallas was more farmers and later, bankers. It seemed more prestigious to be from Dallas, no matter which one won the midsummer Fastest-Egg-Fried-On-The-Sidewalk Contest.)

I'd have kids with names like Cherylynne and Talmadge Wesley. It would take at least six to use up the wonderful names I'd picked out, in spite of the fact I had no interest in kids themselves. They were just an essential part of the fantasy, like a big old house and servants, you had kids because it was unthinkable not to, the drama was irresistible, it was natural, and who would take care of you in your old age?

I came home one afternoon in the fall of that year, a sophomore in high school, shed my school clothes for 'play clothes' kept in the bottom drawer of the dresser, then heard the doorbell ring. Our mailman held out a special-delivery letter for me, a first in my life. Inside was a type-written letter from the Public Relations Manager of a big department store in Dallas, A. Harris, informing me I had won first prize in the regional Seventeen Magazine Save The Children Christmas Federation Doll Making Contest. Enclosed was a $25.00 gift certificate from the department store, and a note that my gift from the magazine, a set of Kromex pantryware, was on the way.

I was bewildered and shocked. I'd never entered a contest or made a doll and didn't know how to sew. What the hell did it mean? (Cussing was in secret vogue as a stress reliever even in childhood. Hell and damn were the only ones we used, although we'd heard Goddamn. Goddamn was too powerful and risky: you could go to Hell for it according to our grandmother. We had a code word for it because it didn't count against you unless you actually said the real word. The code word was GAAAAW. One day our grandmother, Maemama, said to us with a scary squint I KNOW what you're getting at. So we had to Cool Our Jets for awhile. When our father said it our Mother said Franklin! The Children! And he would Cool His Jets for awhile.)

I went back to my book and waited for Mother to come home. She'd been Mommy until just last year.

When I handed the special-delivery to her she looked surprised, then wary. Mother, what is this? I asked after her long silence. Well, she answered slowly, Don't worry about it. She began to walk away.

Whoa, I said What IS this?

Well, she turned halfway around, face still hidden, Your Aunt might have entered a contest in your name, but I am sure it won't go any further than this, so don't worry about it.

I went on with my busy life for the next few weeks, and actually, I didn't think about it, except a couple of times as I was drifting off to sleep. What I thought about was the last paragraph of the brief letter. It said I am sure that you derived a great deal of happiness out of making your doll and you can be certain that some little girl in our country or in Europe will be thrilled with your gift this Christmas. Again, may I congratulate you and thank you for joining this contest. Something about it made me feel queasy.

It wasn't mentioned again, and in our family you did not discuss anything which had not been mentioned. Children did not Bring Things Up, only adults were allowed to do that. Besides, our Aunt Brandee was an artistic, hyperactive character, always up to something, capers. And she often dragged our mother along – they sometimes referred to themselves as Lucy and Ethyl, Mother being Ethyl.

Then the doorbell rang again one day after school. It was the same sort of scene. I'd gotten home from school earlier than the others and Mother was out driving them to appointments. I went to answer it and was astonished to find a uniformed telegram messenger asking for Miss Penny Watson? He handed me the envelope and I opened it. In caps on telegraph strips glued to the letter page, it read:

CONGRATULATIONS. YOU HAVE BEEN AWARDED FIRST PRIZE IN THE 1956 SEVENTEEN MAGAZINE - SAVE THE CHILDREN FEDERATION CHRISTMAS DOLL CONTEST AT NATIONAL JUDGING HELD TODAY IN NEW YORK. MRS ELEANOR ROOSEVELT, CELESTE HOLM, FASHION DESIGNER EDITH HEAD, AND NATALIE WOOD SERVED AS JUDGES. FOR YOUR PRIZE WINNING ENTRY IN FASHION DOLL DIVISION YOU WIN A SERVICE OF GORHAM STERLING SILVER FLATWARE AND SIX-DAY PRIZE TRIP TO NEW YORK NOVEMBER 3 TO 9. THIS WILL INCLUDE SIGHTSEEING, APPEARANCE ON ED SULLIVAN SHOW AND RECEPTION IN YOUR HONOR AT UNITED NATIONS. TRAVEL ARRANGEMENTS AND ACCOMMODATIONS WILL BE MADE FOR YOU. MOTHER OR DESIGNATED CHAPERONE IS INVITED TO ACCOMPANY YOU. PLEASE WIRE ACCEPTANCE COLLECT=SINCERELY

JEAN BAER PUBLICITY DIRECTOR SEVENTEEN MAGAZINE

488 MADISON AVENUE NEW YORK 22 NY=

I felt queasy again, and this time I was on pins and needles waiting for her to get home.

Ah, she sighed. This is actually wonderful news. Your Aunt Brandee entered a DOLL contest. She made three entries, one in your name and two more in her daughter's

names. And, ahhhh, it looks as if the one in your name won.

I thought: Daddy will be home soon and he will fix this. This is crazy.

But Daddy came home and Mother met him at the door. They had one of those closed-bedroom door talks and he came out and said what a lucky girl I was to have this honor. Then he said We won't mention Aunt Brandee's part in it to the other children. They're too young to understand, you know.

They were ages thirteen, eleven and nine. They knew the difference between a lie and the truth. Besides, I was fifteen and I didn't understand it.

He went on, In fact, you must not mention Aunt Brandee's involvement in this to ANYONE, ever. Not your best friends, teachers, anyone at all.

I said But I didn't make it and I don't know how to do it.

Daddy said Your mother and aunt will take care of that. Brandee is arriving tonight and tomorrow afternoon you'll be excused from your last two classes. You have an interview with a reporter from the newspaper. Here's your reply to Seventeen Magazine. He gave me a hug and handed me a note. It said:

I APPRECIATE YOUR HONORING ME. I ACCEPT WITH HUMILITY.

Daddy knew how to make bullshit classy. He'd run for city council – and won- on the slogan Honesty and Integrity. And he was right about the humility part; I felt humble as dirt.

Aunt Brandee showed up about dark. Her red hair glowing, green eyes sparkling, a 'soxy' (her word) low-cut sweater which was a force unto itself. We had dinner and then the other kids were put to bed a bit early before Lucy and Ethyl went into action. As soon as they were sure that everyone was tucked in, they pulled me into the den, sat me down and turned on a bright light to make sure I was alert. I was alert, all right. Queasy and alert.

Mother said I want you to listen very carefully to your Aunt. Brandee said Well, here's the thing: You DIDN'T make the doll, but you COULD HAVE. I'm sure you could have, if you knew how to sew and paint like I do, and even though the doll was in the top 500 winners out of 45,000 entries. In fact, PROBABLY none of the other winners made their dolls. They're just kids!

I closed my eyes. Mother asked quickly Are you having a sinking spell? Do you need a soda cracker? She's a good mother, I thought, and I knew it. The problem was her evil older sister who led her around like.........I dunno. I ate the soda cracker and sipped the coffee they said would help me concentrate. I don't remember having coffee before and it made me shake. I didn't sleep for the next few days, going over the details they drilled into me that night.

YOU got a sock kit for twenty-five cents with a pattern to cut out the arms and legs and body of the doll. You cut them a little curvier because she's a fashion doll. YOU wanted her to be wearing hose so YOU tore up a sheer nylon stocking and stitched stockings over her legs and feet and THEN YOU made the high heels, which are silver and toeless, with matchsticks trimmed down and covered in silver cloth glued on for the heels. It was all way beyond me. YOU decided on a pink georgette fiesta dress – with rows of miniature silver ric-rac, two petticoats – oh, the petticoats are alternating tiers of horsehair and nylon which you bought in the basement of FabricWorld at a sale in August two years ago. (I would have been thirteen then. Amazing.)

Wait a minute – is this the doll you asked me to pose with in the back yard at your house last spring? The one you said was going to be a surprise for cousin Pam?

Yep. She said, whipping a polaroid photo out of her purse, here you are. It will be running in the newspaper in a couple of days. Good thing I thought of that: YOU posing with YOUR doll.

By the way, she continued, a plastic mask came with the doll kit for the face part, but YOU repainted the whole thing. Her bracelet is a silver and turquoise ring cut and shaped with jeweler's tools like her earrings. She has a tiny silver handbag you can't really see in the picture. The picture was slightly fuzzy and I had to memorize all the parts of the doll I couldn't see in the photo. I was blown away by the fact she'd tricked me into posing with the doll six months ago, so casually and secretively I believed it was a gift for her daughter. Aunt Brandee lived a couple of hours away and so there was no follow-up and I'd forgotten all about it. I really wasn't interested in dolls anymore.

Remember last summer when your three best friends went to that two week camp and you had measles? THAT'S when YOU made the doll. You just forgot to mention it to them. I actually did this, and, bless their hearts, my three best friends, Harriet, Liz and Connie, dropped the subject immediately. One of their mothers, however, did not. Chlodine smelled a rat and quizzed me periodically until she saw I couldn't be broken. I'm sure she pieced together the evidence and figured it out.

And guess what – my mother broke in. We're going to make a matching dress for you to wear on the Ed Sullivan show! We already have the pink georgette and forty yards of silver ric-rac! I'm going to let you wear my silver concho belt, turquoise heishi and squash blossom earrings. We have to find you some silver high heels.......

I squinted at the fuzzy picture and thought I might throw up the soda cracker. My mother had been dressing me my whole life, in clothes she made herself. Each night she would come into my room and pick out what I should wear to school the next day. Her specialty, for holidays and family occasions involving crowds, were mother- and daughter costumes. They were either completely identical or in our designated colors, so there would be four of us dressed alike. Mother always looked better than her daughters in the mother-daughter dresses. She loved it when people asked teasingly Now, which one is the mother? Of course it was really obvious which was the mother - the one with the figure! The woman sure knew how to whittle down the competition.

Whenever Aunt Brandee got into the act, the clothes would be over the top and involve ball fringe, rhinestones, or multiple yards of ric-rac. Our father was strict about preferring a classic look, but he was out of town a lot, and occasionally the two sisters just overwhelmed or surprised him. Plus, he was trying to please a beautiful woman half his age who had the whole burden of four children and the household while he traveled and fooled around. He made rules concerning socks (white only) and sheets (no prints or colors allowed), but otherwise he was smart enough to sacrifice us to the good of The Cause: keeping peace. Once he sort of stood up for me. In Junior High I was sent home one day because my dress was cut too low. My mother, furious, wearing a low-cut dress of her own design and a fetching sight, marched into the principal's office. She fixed him with an eagle-eye and said I MADE her dress and it IS appropriate, Sir! He backed down, but she did not choose it for me to wear again to school, although she indignantly insisted I model it for Daddy to get his support after the fact, on his next visit home. Daddy said Lean over, I want to see if they fall out. I wanted to crawl under a rock. I never chose a garment for myself until after I was married.

And now I was going to be on the Ed Sullivan show in one of Lucy and Ethyl's creations, dressed identically to a doll.

Really.

And there was a tie-in to charity: it was a UNICEF project involving milk for babies world-wide and Christmas dolls for underprivileged children. I was, along with the other two top national winners, going to be given a reception at the United Nations, presented with a citation for humanitarian services and a gold medal. I was going to be on Dave Garroway's show and the Virginia Graham show as well as Ed Sullivan's. There were a couple of radio shows, and other stuff. I was going to be famous for something I didn't do.

Yep.

Well, I knew that fame, in the Big Picture, wouldn't last long, except in Wichita Falls. Where I lived. GAAAAW!

THE BEAN FACTORY

The bean factory was a bit of privet hedge growing beneath my bedroom window, on the south side of the house. It was a scrappy and unsuccessful remnant of someone's dream of a hedge, perhaps the former owner, who had been widowed. Between the bush and the house was a small space, about two feet, of cool shade and bare dirt where one could hide from the world, scrunched up small, or play together feverishly all afternoon. It would not shelter you in a game of hide and seek, being too well-known to each of us, but as a private retreat or a bit of bean-counting, it had no equal in the Watson yard.

A few scratchy privet limbs covered the entrance to the hollowed center of the bush, where you sat in a circle of green leaves around and above, with your back to the cool brick wall of the house shaded by the little hedge. The twisted small brown trunk was just to the left and showed a hole in itself about 12 inches above the ground. If you dropped a pinto bean into that hole it would fall out neatly, after a long and mysterious delay, into a small hollow at the roots about three or four inches from the ground, with a satisfying tiny plop. If you had a little dish, say from your dolls' tea set, or the lid of a tin can, the sound became louder and more businesslike. We had all been taken to see the assembly line at our father's factory and were fascinated by it.

Dried peas were too small, butterbeans too big, lima and navy beans somehow uninteresting to us. Besides, pinto beans were the only common sort in that country, also known as "chili beans," and so they were the easiest to hike from the kitchen. Usually it wasn't necessary to steal because our mother was generous with any supplies which kept us busy in the yard. We'd ask her for stuff to make mud pies with and she'd gratefully give us a bit of flour, some ground coffee (coffee beans were unknown), sugar (on a really good day) and a big old metal spoon, slightly bent or dented, and a tough bowl of some kind not too needed in the kitchen or a pot missing its handle. We got water from the outside hose, or straight from the outside faucet by the back door, where the mint grew. We decorated mud pies with cedar berries and mint leaves, small pebbles, and supposedly, pinto beans. Since she seldom saw the finished product or gave them more than a too-busy glance, she did not seem to notice the missing beans. It was not really a deception - she'd have given us a handful of dried beans for the bean factory if we had asked, but some things are just too hard to explain to an adult. She'd want to know what the bean factory was, where it was, whether it was safe and why we would spend our time in such a silly way. She might take a good long look at the stunted privet bush and start thinking about flower beds, where we were not allowed to dig. An unspoken and complicated understanding of the ways of grownups bonded us into a silent conspiricy protecting the bean factory.

Years later when a new air-conditioning system was installed and a big metal-enclosed machine took the ground once graced by the bean factory and we, now teenagers, looked at each other in obvious dismay, our parents were amazed that place meant anything to us. A loud hum filled the air where we had played in intense, sweet solitude and togetherness with the exciting occasional landing of a bird on the bush above your head, a fluttering rustling. How long the bird would stay and how much of the bird you could see from below depended strictly on how still you could be, and this usually depended on how long you could hold your breath. If the bird sang, you felt like God. "The Bean Factory!" we cried out raggedly that day the loud, ugly machine roared into our lives, in unison we grieved: "The Bean Factory is gone!" And it was too late already. Our parents said, "What on earth are you talking about?", having expected us to be as thrilled as they were with automatic, thermostatic cooling. If they ever knew anything about the bean factory it had been long forgotten in the welter of four childhoods twined into one long one. None of us had visited the bean factory for years, simply because we outgrew it. Literally, we couldn't fit into the cozy round space inside the hedge anymore. We did not outgrow our needs for solitude and busyness, of course, and had to find new sorts of bean factories to fill that space where once, with only a handful of dried beans and a hole in a sickly privet trunk, we became masters of commerce, manufacturers, dropping them carefully one by one slowly down the "chute," each disappearing, and then reappearing. In between those points of entry and emergence we imagined a huge gallery of machinery, run by tiny beings who transformed the beans. Although they appeared to be unchanged, we knew they were not. They were now beans with untold powers, possibilities and identities. "Another batch ready for shipment!" we'd call out if we were running the bean factory together and there was a shipping department that day, and the youngest would be handed the beans just outside the bush to run them around the privet and deliver them to the ingoing loading dock. The beans were airplanes, ships, cars, balls of ribbon, yards of cloth, amazing toys, or my personal favorite, magic beans. Magic beans could do anything you could think up, and so valuable we could never set a firm price on them. Millions! We said each one was worth millions of dollars. I have never owned anything so valuable since, nor so coveted, although all this was in our minds, the power and value of magic beans and the process by which they were transformed in the peace and brilliance of the Bean Factory.

PECOS PERVERT PATROL

The time is 11am, the day before Mother's Day. I cruise up the canyon enjoying the spring beauty. The campground at Terrero is full of mothers and children camping – and a shirtless man standing by a beige and gold van with the door open. The man sees me, drops pants, picks up penis and - looking straight at me - he wiggles it. I go into shock and drive a little way before I get mad. I make a quick u-turn and look back across the river. Man does the same thing again. This time I keep going back home, ten miles down the canyon, where female friends insist I report the incident. One friend, however, says Don't worry about it! After tea in the garden tomorrow morning we'll just go up there and find that little weasel.

That was so simple and supportive I felt a lot better, never for a moment taking her seriously. So I answered, Okey-Dokey, anything else? She says Yeah. I made rhubarb cake. And I say I'll be there early then, put on the chai tea. I mean to say, we were just normal, nothing was premeditated, I swear.

We lingered over tea with the garden at its best, fountain splashing, rhubarb cake made by Sharla's mother's recipe, but right after the other ladies left and we brought the dishes back to the kitchen, my hostess comes out with a clip-loaded Glock pistol in a cute little case and says Let's RIDE.

Something came over me – perhaps, I think, the spirit of a long-dead outlaw horse-thief barn-burning ancestor, and I got into her truck without even changing out of my linen tea frock.

On the way up the canyon, steering with her elbows and with the gun propped on top of the steering wheel, my pal shows me how to pop a shell into the chamber. I think maybe she is a little excited because we are going 45 around hair-pin turns with a thousand foot drop on one side and sheer rock crowding the other – but I thought I should concentrate on the gun lesson and didn't mention it. We came up behind a guy who jerked straight up when he looked in his rearview mirror, then quickly pulled over and put his face in his hands like he was praying – but maybe he was just having a bad day.

We get up close to Terrero and I start worrying and say Hey, listen – don't shoot him before I identify him, okay? Thelma (by now we're calling each other Thelma and Louise) asks How you gonna do that? I explain Well I never saw his face. You got to hold the gun on him and make him drop his pants. Thelma complains, all whiney, THEN can I shoot a hole in it?

I'm starting to think my buddy has some serious issues but I just say Of course, Dear, thinking actually how much I'm gonna miss her rhubarb cake while she's away doing time in the Big House and hoping I won't be anywhere around her in there. I personally believe being cell-mates might put a strain on our relationship.

She made a happy little wave in the air with the gun and a guy driving behind us swerved over and screeched to a halt. It looked like he was praying, too. It occurred to me we had become completely different people in the last fifteen minutes without even thinking about it.

Suddenly we were there, at the scene of the crime and, unbelievably, a beige and gold van was parked there. Thelma screams Duck! Duck! There it is! Get down! Don't look! I'm not looking either! I'm headin' for the camp road! When she lets me up again we're cruising past the van and parking below a hill behind it. I get out and with a pink post-em note and pencil in hand, stooped over like a Combat Regular on surveillance, crawl up and write down the license number. Then I get mad and yell in a real mean voice ANYBODY IN THERE? It was so mean it scared me and I ran back to the truck hollering DRIVE, THELMA, DRIVE! She did, and as we pulled away the guy popped out of the van in underwear (Thelma swore it was ladies panties) and ran towards us...but we were hell for leather headed up the canyon, rounding the curve up towards Cowles when we spot a forest service truck coming down. Thelma veered her truck wildly across his lane, arm out the window waving wildly and screaming STOP! STOP!

Deputy Jones managed not to hit us head-on and got out of his truck. He had to bend over until his breathing became regular. When the dust settled we gave him our report and the van license number.

FOREST SERVICE DEPUTY JONES REPORT: MAY 13, 2001, 1:10 pm:

While descending curve to Terrero post office oncoming driver blocks road, honking, yelling and waving arm out of window. Two women scream that they need help immediately. They reported that one of them sighted a semi-naked man the day before who obviously wasn't sunbathing. Apparently the alleged suspect dropped his pants while the victim was looking in his direction, twice. One of the two subjects blurted out We have a gun and we're gonna shoot him! The other one butted in and said No we don't! And if you find him shot we didn't do it, Okay? Subjects give me the license number and description but got into an argument as to whether the van was echru, or beige and gold. I proceed to Terrero campground, radioing Deputy Martinez at Jack's Creek Campground, eight miles up.

FOREST SERVICE DEPUTY MARTINEZ REPORT ON TERRERO INCIDENT MAY 13, 2001 2 pm:

Sighted: Two female subjects driving in wild loops around Jack's Creek Campground. Receive garbled report

WATCHDOG

from Terrero Campground Deputy Jones and radio call from campground host announcing I am needed immediately at his headquarters. Subjects are waiting for me there. They report incident on preceding day at Terrero and tell me to wipe grin off face. I apologize and take report. Female called Louise is the victim. She was unable to describe the alleged perpetrator except to say he appeared to be right-handed. I inquired if that was due to the way he was handling things and they both got mad again. I requested their full names and they initially refused to answer. Finally the victim said Well HER name is Sharla and Sharla said Well HER name is Goose and they had a heated discussion about ratfinks and chickenshits which ended only when I read them their rights and made them hand over their driver's licenses which listed their names, seriously, as Goose Fedders and Sharla Mane. I ordered them to proceed quietly down the mountain and allow the law enforcement to do our own job. Arriving in Terrero I found that Deputy Smith had identified the van and suspect drove away while Smith was radioing me for back-up. There were also three reports on the canyon road of two women wielding a firearm and driving recklessly.

There were no other incidents reported this Mother's Day 2001, except that I am putting in early for retirement. I can't take the excitement anymore.

POISON CONTROL

It happened on a Friday afternoon. I was cleaning the cabinet we lived in, a 12 by 16 foot room we'd built out in the country, a hot still day with insects screeching from the pinon trees. The cabinet was too small to qualify as a cabin, and we had a rule that if one of us stood up the other one had to sit down. While wiping the round table I saw a small paper cup of clear liquid sitting there. I was thirsty so I picked it up and sniffed it – no smell at all – so it must be water. I tossed it down my innocent gullet and went back to wiping. Just seconds later I noticed a strange feeling - something crawling up the inside of my throat. I stood still as I contemplated this ominous sensation, just as my husband Dan opened the door from outside and asked, "Hey, where's that peroxide I was soaking my infected finger in?" And as I opened my mouth in horror the something crawling up inside my throat reached my mouth and spilled out in a froth of bubbles. There was no relief, though, the crawling continued. "Arrrggghhh!" I mumbled through the bubbles to Dan: "I think I just drank it."

"Holy crap." He grabbed a dishtowel so I could catch the next wave of drool pushing out of my mouth, asking "WHY?" and "What do you mean, you THINK?"

"Well, I was thirsty and I thought it was water and it was on the table – oh, never mind – do you think it will kill me?"

"I have no idea! But we've got to DO SOMETHING about it right now."

So I called Poison Control. I'd had the number for years, having survived a wild thrill-seeking teenager whose pockets and backpack I went through every time he took a shower. Then if I found anything suspicious I'd call Poison Control and get them to help me identify it. The teenager frowned on this activity mightily, but we were on a little more equal footing at that point.

They answered and I said, between bubbles and fits of drooling and after identifying myself by name and phone number, "I accidentally drank some peroxide and need to know what I should do now."

"Are you depressed?" the voice asked. "Are you trying to commit suicide?"

"Oh, hell NO! I burbled through the bubbles, which were becoming more and more productive. "I thought it was water."

"Okay," the voice continued. "Well. Well, we've never had anyone report this particular thing before. Are you conscious?"

"I THINK so," I answered carefully. "Would I know if I weren't?" Suddenly I was afraid I might die while talking to a nitwit on the phone.

"Probably not." The voice sounded thoughtful. "It's not listed as a poison but we have no idea what the results would be from drinking peroxide. What is happening now?"

"Well, this shit is crawling up my throat until my mouth is full of bubbles and pressure until I have to open it and hold a towel under my chin to catch this incredible amount of drool. If I keep my mouth closed it leaks out the corners of my mouth and so on and on….and on."

"Okay" the voice said "we've decided we should keep a 24 hour watch on you to see what the symptoms do. We will be calling you every two hours to get a report. But you should call us if anything changes for the worse. Is there someone with you?"

"Yeah, my husband who had been soaking his…..well, never mind, yeah, he's here."

"Have him call us if you lose consciousness. And, uh, try to be careful, Okay?"

I hung up.

We'd made plans to meet a couple we didn't know well at the Steaksmith bar for a drink in an hour. I talked myself into believing that the bubbles crawling up my throat would be long gone by the time we got there. I tried sopping up the foam with tissues all the way there and landed with a soggy handful of dripping wet stuff and no place to put it. I found a bandana in the car and substituted that for the Kleenex I finally stuffed into the side pocket of the car, forgot it and emitted a gargled little scream when I found it on the way home unexpectedly. I felt like a lab experiment gone awry, and made up a story about terrible, terrible allergies for our guests, assuming they actually believed my sinuses are located in my throat. It was a long, long couple of hours of delicately and hopefully unobtrusively dabbing rivulets of endless soda water coursing between the corners of my mouth and my chin with the bandana. Ordering a scotch and soda turned out to be a major mistake: it almost doubled the output of the peroxide, which had apparently become a warm self-perpetuating volcano in my stomach. I didn't dare wonder what lay ahead when it might trigger some sort of self-cleaning action. It was a huge relief to mumble a wet, sloppy goodbye to the bewildered couple and get home to call into poison control with our latest report. About midnight I resigned myself to lying on my stomach so I wouldn't drown in my sleep, the frothing slowed to a drizzle and Poison Control decided we could safely give up the watch over me. By morning all symptoms were gone but for a strange taste in my mouth. I hoped never to need to call Poison Control again.

But about six months later a second incident happened. It was winter now, and coming on to dusk again. A few weeks before I'd decided, in yet another futile effort to rein in my own wild, thrill-seeking nature, that I could only have one cup of coffee a day, so I went to Ohori's in Santa Fe and bought the biggest cup they had for sale. I'd fill it up in the morning and sip it all day long, with repeated trips to the microwave to heat it up. Along about sunset I got to the bottom of the cup, wherein lay a strange insect. It looked like a large black widow spider, except it was a sickly, bleached-out off-white. The hourglass on it was a pale pink. It had to have been in the cup all day long, embalmed in caffeine and cream and honey. That's probably why I didn't notice the poison taste. My uncle's mother had died young from a black widow spider bite. I felt a little dizzy, dizzy enough to consider calling Poison Control, which I had fervently hoped never to have to do again in my lifetime after the peroxide fiasco. While I dialed, I concocted a plan to avoid giving them my name.

"Hello?" I said breathlessly when someone answered perkily "Poison Control here."

"Hello!" I sped up my drawl so it was at least half-normal speed and launched quickly into my situation to discourage any questions from the other end: "I just need to know what might happen if a person accidentally got a black widow spider in their coffee cup and sipped on it all day long?"

There was a very long silence on the line. Finally the voice from Poison Control asked gently, "Is this Goose?" Let me tell you that was a low point in a bad day. It is hard enough to fear you have killed your own ass in a totally freak accident without someone letting you know your reputation has preceded you. The name Goose does not help one bit. I tried to entertain the thought that perhaps northern New Mexico just does not have much poison activity, so I stood out in a sparse crowd, but what with the combo of desert and mountains combined with flash floods, record lightning strikes, rattlesnakes, scorpions, centipedes, brown recluse and black widow spiders, bears, mountain lions, drunk driving and high drug activity, that scenario did not play well. In fact, for many years I'd had a horror that my obituary might bear the headline: Woman Dies in Mishap.

"Well, yes, it is – or I am. Goose, that is. Have we spoken before?"

The answer came hesitantly "No, but I've…ah, heard of you. How are you feeling right now?"

Stupid is how I felt, probably not a symptom of spider-bite, so I said, "Not too good. Whaddya think?"

"Well, Goose, we don't know. Once again, we've never had a problem like this before. How long were you sucking on that cup of coffee?"

"About eight hours." Why did it feel like I was in a dream game of strip poker, my stupidity being exposed one question at a time?

"And, ah, you never saw the spider?"

"Nope. Couldn't see to the bottom of the cup. It is a big cup."

"How big?"

"Well, about 16 ounces. It's Italian."

"Really! Where do you find a cup that big?"

"Ohouri's. Listen, could you try to find out how caffeine affects spider poison? I think I'm having a sinkin' spell."

"Oh, certainly. We're so sorry this happened, Goose. Would you mind speaking to the director of Poison Control, who just happens to be here and has asked us to alert him if you ever…well, would that be all right?"

"Yeah, Sure. Of course." I might as well die while trying

to explain myself, my own sorry ass, to some stranger. It had probably been in the cards all along.

Long story short, they put me on 24 hour watch again with instructions to call in every two hours if okay, which passed uneventfully, except for the wild dreams I experienced that night, and a kind of lowdown feeling the next day which might have been ego-related. For several weeks I was on the lookout for black widow spiders in the cabinet, and saw nothing but my pet Daddy Longlegs who came out whenever I showered and then was eaten by the Venus flytrap I foolishly put into the shower window. I didn't miss him for the first couple of days and then my suspicions fixed on the flytrap and I saw the shadow of my Daddy Longlegs' body inside a leaf with his long legs twitching up in the air. A day later when the legs were unbelievably still jerking I couldn't stand the long agony of the spider any longer and tried to pry apart the leaf with all my strength and could not. I acquired a lot of spider respect that month.

I have not since called Poison Control, but the curse was still upon me. In the spring I took my tattered ego for a rest to Ojo Caliente Hot Springs. I mentioned to a friend on the way that I'd forgotten to bring shampoo and she gave me a hotel sample from her travels. It was in a shiny foil wrapper. Once in the shower at Ojo, shared with about six other women, all strangers to me, I decided to shampoo and could not get a grip on the little packet to tear it open. I tried to rip it open next with my front teeth, with no luck. Finally, I put the foil wrapper between my back molars and bit down hard. It had been a very long time since I was a little kid and learned the hard way about silver fillings and foil coming into contact with each other, so it came as a real shock when I electrocuted myself in the shower. I jumped off the floor and screeched an inhuman sound, a muffled WHARRRGGGHHHHEEEEEEE! As the electrical current went from the back of my throat to my feet and simultaneously the foil packet burst open as my teeth clamped down convulsively, squirting half the shampoo directly down my throat while the other half flew out of the end hanging out of my mouth. The six other women, whom I would have liked to think of as my sisters in womanhood stared at me, turned away as one and left the shower.

The dressing room was empty by the time I'd cleaned up the mess and gotten out, hair still unwashed because I'd swallowed most of the shampoo. Calling Poison Control didn't even cross my mind. I didn't care anymore.

My body was tired but my mind was even more so, and after a solitary dinner in the Springs dining room during which not one of the other guests spoke to me, I slept well until about midnight when I woke up and burped a big iridescent bubble.

When my daughter made her weekly call to check on me I told her about the silly incident with a giggle, saying "Can you believe I did such a goofy thing?"

"Yes," she answered promptly, "Remember the garlic removal episode?"

I DID remember it, and rued the knowledge that someone was keeping track of my little rough patches. It had happened when she was a child, and I had assumed she would forget it with the years, or at the very least would not be unkind enough to bring it up. I'd had a yeast infection and researched it in my Mother Earth Home Remedy book, since the Bach Flower Remedy system did not deal with such problems. I was so happy when the book informed me the simple remedy was just a garlic clove inserted into the vagina! Aha! I knew I could outsmart the whole Western medicine requirements myself. I raced to the kitchen and quickly applied the remedy in the bathroom.

All was well for almost twenty minutes until I noticed that the odor of garlic was wafting from every pore in my body. It was so strong my eyes were watering. I raced back to the Home Remedy Book, opened it up and turned the page. That's when I saw that I had not finished reading the instructions for applying the garlic. The garlic was supposed to be wrapped in a long strip of gauze with a tail hanging down so that it could be removed easily. OR AT ALL. Two days later, having spent forty-eight hours in a garlic fog, I sat in the doctor's office after the Western procedure for removal of garlic from the reproductive tract and asked the doctor what exactly he was writing on my chart. "Removal of garlic," he answered.

"I really don't want that on my chart!" I complained.

"Well, Goose," he replied, "In that case, you should have finished the chapter in the book."

In closing and on the theme of protective self care, I would like to caution you all not to shoot off a slingshot inside your vehicle, as well as not drinking peroxide, boiling and drinking a poisonous spider or putting a clove of garlic up your twat.

The circumstances, which occasion this warning, involve a neighbor who had moved his chained-up dog

out of my throwing reach for treats. I must put up with some injustice in this world, but not that. In a hardware store I ran across a good slingshot, rather more powerful than the homemade ones we had as kids. I cruised to my best position for firing a treat to my canine buddy and aimed through the passenger side window, clearly my first big mistake, other than being there to start with. Holding one arm straight out, I pulled the sling back as far as I could and my arm made a tiny wobble to the right just as I let fly. The dog treat chunk hit the center post between the car windows going about the speed of light and began a process called RICOCHET, bouncing back across the car at lethal speed a half-inch from my sunglasses before it hit the driver's side window and shot across my nose and missing it by a quarter-inch into the windshield before launching into the rear windshield, nicking the glass and shooting forward again to whack me in the back of my head. In the preceding second and a half I had nearly been blinded, broken my nose and been knocked half unconscious by a chunk of dog food. It could easily have been in the Guinness Book of World Records for innovative but unreliable ways to kill and/or maim oneself. If it had actually gone through the open window it could have killed the dog. It being me. I think that guy at the hardware store should not have sold me that slingshot without a background check involving Poison Control and a sobriety test just in case. I was also overage to be purchasing a slingshot. Clearly overage. I thought the next best thing to do was go home, as quietly as possible and lie down until the double vision went away.

Goose Pâté

Speaking of that, I don't have double vision anymore. I'm lucky to have any vision at all since my cataract surgery when I got the little eye drop bottle confused with a very similar small dropper bottle of - there's no way to soften this – super glue. And all I have left to say is: Don't do that either. I couldn't see to dial Poison Control, but I had memorized the number by then.

Tame Yo' Hog

OR

How To Make a Silk Purse From a Sow's Ear

As a storyteller, I find a bit of fantasy enriches inspiration, so I've used the idea presented here to help make up a story in which it is easier to see our world and ourselves. It is a story about how to manage problems, bad habits in particular. Uncountable words have been written and spoken by therapists to help people identify their problems and deal with them.

My expertise in this field does not include credentials or education, but the experience of a long life, decades of reading self-help books, years of personal therapy, several crazy family members, lots of nut-ball friends, 50 years residence in northern New Mexico and some dog training. My notions are valid and techniques are simple and non-toxic – the reader takes little risk to decide to try on my fantasy idea and see if it fits. I probably don't know more about hogs than the average person, but my grandmother did, and I listened – and before you snort at that (a hog-like proclivity) stop and think: it all counts in life.

CHAPTER ONE: ACKNOWLEDGE YO' HOG

I had an uncle who said "Everybody's got their own sack of rocks to carry around." He meant their problems and bad habits. But I feel that problems and bad habits are much more lively than a sack of rocks. They have energy of their own, counter to your own good sense and goals. Think of them as your hogs. They are not yourself, and you are not they – yet, there is a clear connection to you: like third cousins twice removed, recognizable, related, but not essential. Still, they are present, and must be dealt with.

Oh, yeah, we've all got one, a HOG running loose behind the scenes, like dirty laundry on the line. Hogs start small, as cute little piglets who sneak candy and pee in swimming pools and pick their noses – but they get bigger, and fast.

Folks, porcine proclivities are part of the human condition, like noses and bullshit. There is no 'if' you have a hog, you HAVE it and IT'S A HOG. A piglet gone to hoggery and all sorts of hog mischief.

CHAPTER TWO: WHO'S YO' HOG?

In reality, if you think for a second, you know yo' hog and its manners, what it likes too much and constantly bugs you about. You got to IDENTIFY yo' hog, call out its name and teach it some manners or it will continue to hog out yo' life.

There's a hog loose in your spare time, maybe, and it just wants to lay down on the floor, smoke dope, drank hooch 'n EAT. Maybe it's a pious hog that overexercises and avoids loved ones that way, or a party hog, out every night. There are church hogs and golf hogs and – you-name-it - you get the picture. There could be a hog loose in your memory, just digging up crap instead of truffles, a bad-spirited ole hog. There are social hogs, musician hogs, artist hogs, political hogs: the bottom line is that they care about their thang above all else. Especially above you. DON'T FEED THAT HOG! It's had enough. IT'S A HOG, and hogs can be mean. That hog is not your friend or your enemy. They flat-out just don't give no nevermind.

Therefore, emotions, good or bad, about yo' hog, are a waste of time. Give your own self a good hug, and thank your self for being on your own side, try not to worry about talking to yourself, and set about TRAINING that hog.

CHAPTER THREE: DINNER WITH A HOG?

Don't be taking yo' hog out to dinner or the movie-show or whatever it likes the best. YOU can go, but leave that hog at home so it won't be snorting around you wanting more, more, more. That way you can relax, and a little becomes a lot. Close the door on that hog. Fence it in with rules.

Watch out for other people's hogs. There are nice ways to suggest they not bring their hogs to dinner, or over to your house. When you are getting yo' hog under control, don't get eat up by somebody else's hog.

CHAPTER FOUR: GETTING AHOLD OF YO' HOG

Here's the deal: If you can see yo' hog, you can tame it. Otherwise, yo' hog may just sneak up behind you and take over. This is why you got to be the boss of it. Accept the job and tame yo' hog!

Don't go into hog denial or claim 'yo' hog made you do it. We TRAIN hogs and TEACH people, for goodness sake.

Listen up. Believe it or not, yo' hog can come to enjoy spinach salad in time instead of slop. Add a handful of almonds and cranberries. No, this advice is not in most self-help books, but the idea is to make enough small healthy concessions to make big changes tolerable. I once read a diet which said to have an apple and a twenty minute walk for lunch. I snorted at it but my friend Lucy proceeded to lose twenty pounds doing exactly that, in two months, and she came to love walking. Was her hog surprised! And so was Lucy and so was I. See, big stuff in life WILL happen, but the little stuff is yours to fool around with, and there is great power in it. DO ONE THING DIFFERENT is a book I can recommend for this technique, written by Bill O'Hanlon, who was on the Oprah show with it. My Reading Hog didn't want to read it, in fact refused to read it, which was a sure sign that I SHOULD read it. The Reading Hog just likes fun stuff and People magazine and carefully avoids reading anything which might affect her comfort zone. So I read it, while my Reading Hog snuffled and grunted, and laid out in the sunshine under the window. And I was then one up on my Reading Hog. Ever little bit counts, friend. Another tip, imagine you are writing a book during this process, called HOG, INTERRUPTED.

Someday, when things are well under control, you can take yo' hog to France, but not until after a lot of exercise and discipline. Yes, someday you can reward yo' hog for knowing you are top dog, but not today.

CHAPTER FIVE: HOG INTERVENTION

The Hog Whisperer believes a great tool for getting in touch with yo' hog while holding it at arm's length – is Hog Camp, where friends get together and work on their hogs and empathize. This could be a short getaway or longer if possible. At Hog Camp you don't ignore yo' hogs, but pay close attention to their piggy ways and share whatever has helped you to get them under control. The hogs don't like this, of course, and their protests will show up in various forms of cravings. You can take a little bit of wicked pleasure in their discomfort – turn about is fair play!

But beware – if everyone there is not vigilant the hogs will get together and sneak forbidden items into Hog Camp – chocolate eclairs mysteriously appear from the village down the road, a pipe full of weed, a bottle of Bailey's, a deck of cards with naked ladies on the front. LOL right in yo' hog's happy face when you shitcan that stuff. Don't let them turn YOUR intervention into HOG CITY. Surprise! There is no big hog rebellion, no consequences to their anger, just a grunt and a squinty look.

Yo' hog hogs yo' energy and you got to run it off. Twice a day take yo' hog out on a leash and don't go home til it's too tired to play. Almost never fails, this one.

Imitate yo' hog. This one almost never works, since hogs are hogs, but you can try it for the supportive effect of ritual, and because it will embarrass yo' hog. Go out into the woods and find some leaves under a big tree. Dig a hole and roll, snort and grunt into it. Full moon is best. (Do NOT try this in javelina country, in a barnyard, or if you can hear banjo music.) Go on home then.

CHAPTER SIX: SICK HOGS or When To Make Spam

Some hogs cannot be tolerated. They are just too big and bad and piggy. We need not go into detail here: those of you who harbor a vicious, nasty hog know who you are, and you know when that hog is crowding you right out of your own life. Don't pussyfoot around that hog anymore. Tell it off, open the door wide and enjoy the sight of that hog's gigantic ass thundering down the street, growing smaller and smaller in the dust kicked up by all that badness, until it vanishes forever. Then slam the door and turn on the radio. Remember, yo' hog is not YOU: it's yo' HOG. And if that doesn't work, just kill that hog dead and make some spam and eat it when you are feeling low, with white bread and mayo. That's right, use that hog up in one sandwich. Adios, Porker! It's just a mindset. Fantasies can be good for you, and at least they are legal.

A new piglet will soon appear, for hogs are always with us in life, but it will be a less dangerous one now that you have stood up for yo'self. This little piggy may read too much or jog to extremes or smoke tailor-made cigarettes – some damn thing – but you're in control now. Hogs CAN learn, but talking to them is useless.

CHAPTER SEVEN: As They Say Down On The Hog Farm: You Cured Yet?

Once things are under control, no longer hog-wild or even close to it, you can relax somewhat – although never, ever completely. You can take yo' small, under-control hog to France and have a croissant. Remind yo' hog it is a rare and special treat, and enjoy! Now you're in Hog Heaven, buddy – but tomorrow – NO CROISSANT! Congratulations! You have tamed yo' hog.

Chick Diary

Well, the baby chicks arrived yesterday! We are so excited! They are just the cutest, fluffiest little things. We split fifty chicks with our friend Gwynne and brought them home from the store, to our hand-built alternative space, and built the fire right up, since it is a very cold springtime here. The man at the feed store mentioned that we might have ordered the chicks a bit early for this climate, but we were just so ready to get started we went ahead anyway. He also wanted to sell us some chick feed but of course we knew better. That commercial stuff is probably loaded with chemicals and certainly is not good enough for our barnyard royalty, no sir - we've done our homework reading Mother Earth News magazine and sent off for a recipe and a hand grinder to make our own dear chick feed.

I got right to work grinding up grains and other good stuff while Dan and the kids kept the fire going, but the grinder turned out to be kind of hard to use and takes both hands and all my strength to turn the handle.

However, the chick feed looks just great, although a little more powdery than the stuff at the store. It doesn't stay in the nice little glass dish I provided for them either, since they walk through the pretty little china dish of water I provided and then through the chick feed and it gets all mixed up together.

March 17, 1974

We are still up all night keeping the fire going for the chicks, since the solar aspect of our domicile doesn't seem to work very well in the early spring. I don't know why Mother Earth News didn't mention this. The chicks are making a lot of noise now, but not chirping. They are nosily clumping around in their box as the chick feed, when moistened with their drinking water, seems to form solid and unbreakable balls of concrete around their feet which we can't manage to break off. They aren't eating much of it either. I am experimenting with the grinder to try to get a better consistency. The Home Poultry books we bought don't mention this problem. I suppose they just expect us to buy the chick feed at the store and not bother with making the changes which will ultimately alter our society once people understand things can be done in a better way with a little thought and effort. We've explained to the children that all this work is just part of restructuring the world we all live in, but they still seem a little glum and made some remarks about eating dried lettuce. Well, that was just a little experiment of mine and perhaps they haven't yet fully entered into the spirit of the Seventies here. I really would have expected children of mine to embrace change more joyously. They do seem bonded to the baby chicks, however, and perhaps overly concerned that they are not doing well.

April 13, 1974

The precious little baby chicks mostly died after all, due to a combination of cold weather and poor eating habits - they couldn't get the homemade chick feed off their feet! However, six of them made it and are now residing in their own sweet alternative coop space outside. The children have named all the survivors which the book says not to do if you plan to eat them. However, after all we have been through to raise them we couldn't think of eating them and have decided to become vegetarians, so that problem won't be coming up again. We're planning a big garden with the children, who were so silly, saying they want to plant mangos, lambs and some cows! Aren't they cute? It's going to be a great summer!

Entry by a Chick Survivor:

Ah, Jeez, I'm almost a full day older than most of these chicks who were in the box from the feed store, so I knew right away when these hippie idiots opened our box at their 'alternative home space' that we were in a sucking karmic vortex. First off, they were carrying on as if we were stuffed animals to set on a shelf and look at. The worst news I heard was that they planned to make our own feed for us. Sure enough, the feed - all served out of the wrong type containers, got all mixed up together and bonded like super glue to our feet and we sounded like goose- stepping Nazis in our box. They could have humanely tossed us into a bucket of water for perfect Mafia-style executions, but no, we just staggered around until we pitched over into exhaustion and 'a chance to reincarnate and elevate,' as those alternative nitwits put it. It was a Chicken Bataan Death March, and the children gave the first few lovely little funerals until the novelty wore off. Well, I made it through with a few hardy others and believe me, when I get to the top of this karmic heap as king of the world, I'm gonna make a law that college graduates and readers of Mother Earth News are banned from owning chickens forever.

HEMINGWAY IN PECOS

When we came out of the post office the air had turned sharp. "What do you want to do?" She looked toward the mountain at the controlled burn. "Are you hungry?"

We were already walking towards Frankie's Casanova then. "How about you? I'm a little bit hungry." She said it sweetly, even though we were always hungry that year. While I wrote in the casita she foraged for pinon nuts and windfall apples, ignoring the bear scat. She had told me about it until I felt guilty and angry and then we'd had an argument. I told her to stop it; it would look bad if a bear ate my woman while I was writing short stories, or even a novella. It would make me look weak. But that had been last month and there was no more mention of bears. She was a good wife, a keeper.

"Let's just go in here and have a truly grand dinner," I said, wanting to make it up to her. "Let's have chile rellenos and beer. How about it?"

"That's perfect, and it's so close, Tatie." We ate the rellenos at the smallest and warmest table by the fireplace. Irwin kept poking logs into the fire while the sun went down. Bobwire Bob came in with a blast of freezing air, made three circles clockwise, and went out when Misty yelled at him for letting the heat out. No one else came in and our coats were steaming when we went outside into the moonlight. It was a good night and we would be home before the coyotes came out. We would go to bed and make love, and I would be writing again before the first one howled.

We lived above the beauty shop just off Hwy 63 and it was wonderful to walk down the long flight of stairs knowing that I'd had good luck working. I always worked until I had something done and I always stopped when I knew what was going to happen next. That way I could be sure of going on the next day. I would stand and look out over the flat roofs of Pecos and think, "Do not worry. You have always written before and you will write now. All you have to do is write one true sentence. Write the truest sentence that you know." So finally I would write one true sentence and then go on from there. It was easy then because there was one true sentence that you knew or had seen or had heard someone say. Up in that room I decided that I would write one story about each thing that I knew about. I was trying to do this all the time I was writing, and it was good and severe discipline.

It was in that room too that I learned not to think about anything that I was writing from the time I stopped writing until I started writing again the next day. That way my subconscious would be working on it and at the same time I would be listening to other people and noticing everything, learning - I hoped, and I would read so that I would not think about my work and make myself impotent to do it. That was a big issue for me, still is. Going down the stairs when you had worked well – and that needed luck as well as discipline – was a wonderful feeling and I was free then to walk anywhere in Pecos.

If you are lucky enough to have lived in Pecos as a young man, then wherever you go for the rest of your life, it stays with you, for Pecos is a moveable feast. That is, if you like menudo, the Breakfast of Champions. Menudo is guts, chicos and chile, not for sissies, but only for real men. I ate menudo with the best of them, the locals and, yeah, they noticed. But still, whenever I called out proudly "Buenos dias, Senor (or Senorita)" they would answer sourly "Good morning, Asshole," hurting my feelings. I switched to "Hola, Amigo!" and they answered sourly "Give it up, Gringo." Later on, my friend Eloy told me only Californians say that Hola thing. Eloy will sometimes give me a clue. But then Eustacio told me Eloy is a coyote. I asked Eloy what that means and he said "Chinga tu madre." My Spanish is not perfect, but I understood he was telling me that his mother had mated with a coyote, and I felt sad for him. I would not have brought it up or asked him such a thing if I had known. Eloy is embarrassed now and will not speak to me. This is sad, for we had eaten menudo together many times and toasted each other with Bud Light.

Although I was sad about this, I was still learning. Work could cure almost anything. I believed it then, and I believe it now. Then all I had to be cured of, according to Joyce Depow, was youth and loving my wife. I was not at all sad when I got home to the casita and told my newly acquired knowledge to my wife and we were happy in the night with our own knowledge we already had and other new knowledge we had acquired in the mountains.

STRANGLESS STRANG BANES

This is a story about me and my ole buddy Mr. Blankenship. We talked gardens and bees and tornadoes, and played an occasional prank on one another when the time was right – that is when enough time had gone by that one of us had almost forgotten we were next in line and overdue. This could be tricky, and it was important to be sneaky and patient, so the victim never sees it coming.

I'd got him pretty good after he'd planted his cucumber seeds in tidy little hills and bragged about how big this new hybrid was gonna be. While he was out of town I sliced huge dill pickles in half and pushed then into the hills as if they'd sprouted that way. He said someone had ruined his crop and started over, looking sour and squinty-eyed in my direction. Fact is, he had extra cucumbers that season.

Then I'd found the nearly life-size cow and calf which were silk-screened onto plywood and looked perfectly real from a distance, could not resist and shelled out a week's pay for them. I waited til Mr. Blankenship lay down for his nap and set them up in his garden in the half-growed corn. After awhile I saw the blinds go up

a little ways and heard his little dog start to go crazy yapping, then the blinds popped back down, and the dog shut up. Then he reopened the blinds and the dog charged at the patio door having what Mama called a catty-cornered wall-eyed fit, which repeated itself three times as he tried to get a look at the cows, muttering to himself and hollering at the dog to stay back and shut up. Finally he slammed the blinds shut and went out the front door and off in his truck, yelling out that he needed some ammo for his gun. I spirited away the evidence while he was gone. Them cows was worth every penny.

That was twice in a row for me, but even so and smart as I am, I did not see the next thang coming: that would be the strangless strang banes.

Come spring and Mr. B. put up his bean-pole tipi and tells me he is planting the latest, greatest thang yet: strangless strang banes. Mr. B. and me both hail from Texas and pronounce string as 'strang' and beans as 'banes.' Green banes are the best veggies, except for the drawback of that tough strang you got to pull off before cooking. He asked me if I'd like some of those strangless strang bane seeds to plant in my garden, which he had ordered special from an outfit in California, a brand-new deal. It's a great big old bane, he tells me, three of 'em will serve six at dinner.

Sure thang, I shot back, and you're a damn fool for them seed catalogues every single sprang. But I'll give her a try, anyhow. My pride was somewhat involved since last fall when his pumpkins were huge and mine looked like ornamentals next to his, a fact he mentioned more often than necessary. I produced nine perfect dipper gourds next to his four, but one of his had a knot tied in the stem. The man has a showy nature, that's all I'm saying. He would slide around with some of that bread he baked, just out of the oven, and be telling you how a bee line is made while you ate it. Showy. I believe he may have been born in Oklahoma, but I can't prove it.

Well, the summer passed and the garden was good. Them banes was big, bigger than any banes I ever saw, hanging down a foot and more. Couldn't see no strang on 'em but when harvest time came, it was a different story. I picked a few bright green banes and popped the tip of one into my mouth and bit down ONTO A STRANG. YEP, A STRANG ON A STRANGLESS STRANG BANE AND THE TOUGHEST DARN STRANG EVER, LIKE A DURN ROPE. It slid in between my front teeth and

THE GAME

stuck there while I pulled off about two and a half feet of strangless strang bane. In my mind I could hear that old man laughing as I yanked it out of my mouth. The strangless strang bane was mostly strang, and I had carried water to them suckers all summer long while Lyn Blankenship laughed. But he had given me the seeds and I owed him a thank-you note. Here it is:

Dear Mr. Blankenship,

I want to thank you for your generous gift of the seeds for the strangless strang banes. However, to my surprise they were not strangless strang banes after all, but giant strang banes. I was so amused at your little joke that I began to save the strangs off the strangless strang banes to show you. I began to make a ball. We were just eating strangless strang banes by then anyway since that is mostly all we grew this year, on your advice, and they took over the garden. When I tried to sell them to the fancy cafe in town the chef said strang banes are probably the least popular vegetable and that strangless strang banes sounds even worse on a menu, and besides they weren't even strangless. Well, I knew that.

That ball of strangless green bane strangs just grew and grew and finally I decided to bring it over to show you and was rolling it from the shed to the wagon when it got loose from me and took off down the hill where it rolled over our entire flock of chickens which stuck to it and then slammed into ole Nelly who keeled over onto the milk cow. The chickens quit laying, the cow went dry and then the bank man come by and says You're out. He took ole Nelly with him.

But I digress. Thanks again for the strangless strang banes. They were something else.

Your friend,

Goose

I mailed my note and about a week later ole Mr. B. drops by with a pint of homemade chow-chow and some yard eggs, and told me while I was eating it how to move a wild bee hive, and then shuffled his feet and said Hey, thanks for that poem or whatever it was.

Once again, we were even-steven.

Dear Mr. Blankenship,

I want to thank you for your generous gift of the seeds for the strangless strang banes. However, to my surprise they were not strangless strang banes after all, but giant strang banes. I was so amused at your little joke that I began to save the strangs off the strangless strang banes to show you. I began to make a ball. We were just eating strangless strang banes by then anyway since that is mostly all we grew this year, on your advice, and they took over the garden. When I tried to sell them to the fancy cafe in town the chef said strang banes are probably the least popular vegetable and that strangless strang banes sounds even worse on a menu, and besides they weren't even strangless. Well, I knew that.

That ball of strangless green bane strangs just grew and grew and finally I decided to bring it over to show you and was rolling it from the shed to the wagon when it got loose from me and took off down the hill where it rolled over our entire flock of chickens which stuck to it and then slammed into ole Nelly who keeled over onto the milk cow. The chickens quit laying, the cow went dry and then the bank man come by and says You're out. He took ole Nelly with him.

But I digress. Thanks again for the strangless strang banes. They were something else.

Your friend,

Goose